Swans

By Cameron Macintosh

A swan is a big bird.

Swans swim around rivers and lakes, and in swamps.
They like fresh water better than salt water.

Most swans are black or white,
but some can be both!

Swans have long necks, which they use to find food.
They can use their long necks to reach plants that grow under the water.

Swans like to eat plants, but they also swallow up insects, fish, tadpoles and even frogs.

Swans have big, webbed feet.

They waddle on land, but their feet are good for swimming, too.

The webbing on their feet helps them push through the water.

Swans like to wander around in groups, or squads.

A squad of swans is called a bevy.

Most swans find a mate and stay with them for all their life.

Swans make nests by the water.

They make nests from wads of reeds, leaves and stems.

Then they lay up to eight eggs.

What a great nest!

The mum and dad swans take it in turns to squat over the eggs to keep them safe.
They do not squash them!

They keep the eggs cosy and safe until they hatch.

Baby swans are called cygnets.

Before they learn to swim, cygnets catch a ride on their mum's back!

Watch these cygnets take their first swim!

Watch from far away, though!

Swans do not want you to get close to their cygnets. They will chase you if you do!

This goose was too close to the swan's cygnets.

Swans wash and groom their feathers.

They make a kind of oil at the base of their tails.
The oil protects the feathers from getting too wet.

Swans can fly, too.
In fact, they are one of the biggest flying birds!

Swans are stunning!

CHECKING FOR MEANING

1. Where do swans swim? *(Literal)*
2. What are two facts about swans that you learned from the text? *(Literal)*
3. Why do you think swans don't want you to get near their cygnets? *(Inferential)*
4. Has the author told you everything you want to know about swans? Is there anything else you would like to know? *(Evaluative)*

EXTENDING VOCABULARY

swamps	What is the base of the word *swamps*? What is a swamp like? Where might you find a swamp?
wander	What does it mean to wander? Do you move quickly or slowly if you are wandering? What is another word you know with a similar meaning?
squad	How is the word *squad* used in the text? When might people form a squad?

MOVING BEYOND THE TEXT

1. Some people throw bread to ducks and swans for them to eat, but bread is bad for them. Why should you not feed wild animals?

2. Swans eat both plants and meat, which means they are omnivores. Which other animals are omnivores?

3. What are some other birds that live on the water? What animals live *in* the water?

4. The author said that swans waddle on land. What other words can be used to describe the different ways that swans move?

TIME TO WRITE

Imagine you are a swan. Write about a day in your life. Where do you go? What do you do? What food do you find to eat?